DIRE WO!VES

ASHLEY GISH

ICE AGE CREATURES
X
BOOKS

NORTH
AMERICA

EUROPE

ASIA

AFRICA

SOUTH
AMERICA

AUSTRALIA

T0002397

CREATIVE EDUCATION · CREATIVE PAPERBACKS

Published by Creative Education and Creative Paperbacks • P.O. Box 227, Mankato, Minnesota 56002 • Creative Education and Creative Paperbacks are imprints of The Creative Company • www.thecreativecompany.us • Design by Rita Marshall • Production by Dana Koelke • Printed in the United States of America • Photographs by 123rf (Oksana Desiatkina, Zhanna Tretiakova), Alamy (Chronicle, Heritage Image Partnership Ltd) iStockphoto (Andyworks, breckeni, Dgwildlife, JackF, Vac 1, westcini), Dorling Kindersley, Valentyna Chukhlyebova, DanielMcHenry, Daniel Eskridge, Geoffrey Kuchera, Getty Images (Ted Soqui), Shutterstock (AuntSpray, Joseph Sohm, Svetsol), SuperStock (Jim Brandenburg/Minden pictures), Corbis

DIRE WOLVES

CONTENTS

ICE AGE CREATURES
BOOKS

XCEPTIONAL ANCIENT ANIMALS

Dire wolves lived during the Ice Age. Their scientific name, *Canis dirus*, means "fearsome dog." They walked among mammoths, bison, and saber-toothed cats.

Dire Wolf Basics

Dire wolves are **extinct** relatives of gray wolves. They are part of the Canidae family. This group includes wolves, coyotes, foxes, and dogs. Dire wolves lived in a variety of places. They roamed forested mountains and dry grasslands.

DIRE WOLVES

Dire wolves looked similar to other canids. They had thick fur. Their fur varied in color from black and gray to rusty brown. Their broad heads had upright ears.

NORTH
AMERICA

SOUTH
AMERICA

DIRE WOLVES

lived throughout North

and South America.

DIRE WOLF

GRAY WOLF

Dire wolves had short, powerful legs. They were more
than five feet (1.5 m) long from the tip of their pointed
nose to the end of their bushy tail. They weighed 125
to 175 pounds (56.7-79.4 kg). The largest canid alive
today is the gray wolf. Dire wolves were about 25
percent bigger than the gray wolf. The last dire wolves
went extinct about 10,000 years ago.

NOT PICKY

Dire wolves often ate animals they found dead.

Scientists have found cracks on the remains of dire wolves' back teeth. This suggests that the wolves crushed bones to eat.

Gray wolves and dire wolves lived in the same areas. But they did not compete for food. They ate different animals. Gray wolves hunted deer and other fast prey. Dire wolves took down slower-moving animals, such as ancient bison.

Sometimes, dire wolves and saber-toothed cats fought over food.

Remains of both animals have often been found together.

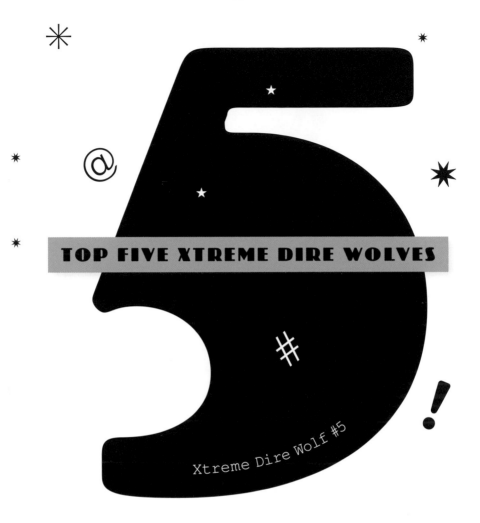

TOP FIVE XTREME DIRE WOLVES

Xtreme Dire Wolf #5

A Unique Foot In 2012, wolf foot bones were discovered near Tule Springs **Fossil** Beds National Monument in Nevada. There are many Ice Age animal fossils in this area. Scientists compared the foot bones to dire wolf and gray wolf bones from other states. The bones were from a dire wolf. It was the first time dire wolf fossils had been found in Nevada.

Dire Wolf Beginnings

Like other wolves, dire wolves were social. They lived in family groups called packs. The pack was led by two wolves. They were the alpha male and alpha female. These wolves were the first to eat after a kill. Many experts believe that only the alpha pair had pups.

Dire wolves dug underground holes, called dens. The alpha female gave birth to her pups in the den. There were probably between one and nine pups, the same number that gray wolves have.

The adults went hunting. Meanwhile, the pups were safe inside their den. Pups grew fast. At first, they drank milk from their mother. After several weeks, they tasted meat. Their mother ate first. Then she would **regurgitate** meat for her pups. This meal was delicious to dire wolf pups! After a few months, the pups left their den. They traveled with the rest of the pack.

12 to **24** days

eyes open, learn to walk, and eat regurgitated meat

8 to **10** weeks

no longer drink milk; leave den and join the rest of the pack

6 months

adult teeth replace milk teeth; follow during hunts

7 to **12** months

actively hunt with pack; fully grown by the end of 12 months

DIRE WOLF BEGINNINGS FACT

Males had bigger teeth than females.

Females were attracted to males with bigger teeth.

TOP FIVE XTREME DIRE WOLVES

Xtreme Dire Wolf #4

Dire Wolves in Fiction Dire wolves appear in books, television shows, and video games. Fictional dire wolves are bigger than the animals on which they are based. *Dungeons & Dragons* game lore describes dire wolves as being 9 feet (2.7 meters) long and weighing 800 pounds (362.9 kg)! In the *Game of Thrones* television series, dire wolves are the size of ponies. Players can ride dire wolves in the video game *ARK: Survival Evolved*.

Dire wolves could bite harder than the largest gray wolves.

XTRAORDINARY LIFESTYLE

The remains of dire wolves and saber-toothed cats have been found at the La Brea Tar Pits in California. These animals were trapped in liquid asphalt while searching for food.

Dire wolves did not give rise to other creatures.

NO DESCENDANTS

Dire Wolf Society

Dire wolves ate lots of meat. They were hypercarnivorous. This means more than 70 percent of their diet was meat. The rest came from plants and berries. Research suggests humans and dire wolves hunted the same kinds of animals. We do not know if competition for food caused dire wolves to die out.

There were two **subspecies** of dire wolves. *Canis dirus guildayi* lived west of the Rocky Mountains. It had short legs. *Canis dirus dirus* lived east of the Rocky Mountains. Its legs were long and slender. It was bigger than its western cousin.

XEMPLARY DISCOVERIES

Scientists look at modern wolves to learn about how dire wolves lived. Today's gray and red wolves have similar traits. They live in packs. They often hunt together. They dig dens for their pups. Dire wolves were similar in many ways to modern wolves.

Some dead animals become **mummified**. These animals give scientists lots of information. The animal's flesh, skin, and fur may be preserved. Many Ice Age animals have been found in **permafrost**. The remains are thousands of years old. But they look like they died recently!

Scientists have not found many dire wolf pup fossils. Pups stayed safe inside their den. But natural disasters like floods and mudslides were dangerous. Pups could have been trapped in their den.

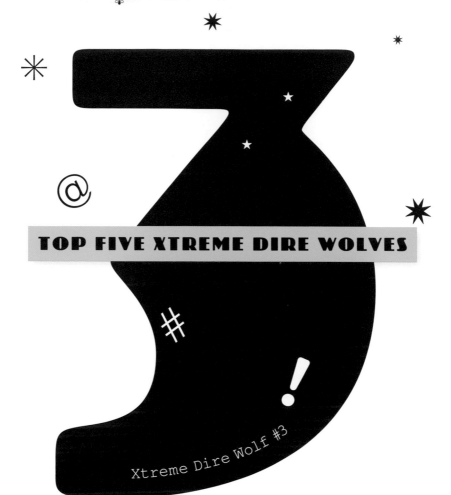

TOP FIVE XTREME DIRE WOLVES

Xtreme Dire Wolf #3

Preserved Pup In 2016, miners looked for gold in the Yukon region of Canada. They found a wolf pup instead. It was more than 50,000 years old. But its flesh, skin, and fur were all preserved. Fossil scientist Grant Zazula noted that it was the only mummified Ice Age wolf in the world. Dire wolves did not range as far north as the Yukon. The pup is likely a gray wolf that died between six and eight weeks of age.

XASPERATING CONFLICT

Dire wolves worked together to keep their pack strong. But they faced many dangers. Dire wolves dealt with deadly asphalt. They competed with other large predators for food.

Dire Wolf Survival

Dire wolves were top predators. They relied on a steady population of slow-moving prey. At the end of the Ice Age, many large plant-eaters became extinct. Dire wolves were not fast enough to catch deer and other swift prey. Researchers believe this may be one reason dire wolves died out.

After an animal dies, it may get covered by water and dirt. If conditions are right, fossils will form from the animal's bones. Scientists study fossils to learn about extinct animals.

In a few cases, scientists have found the remains of injured dire wolves. It looked like their injuries had healed before the wolves died. This led scientists to believe that dire wolves cared for injured pack members. This behavior would have been unique to dire wolves. Other kinds of wolves leave injured pack members behind.

DIRE WOLF SURVIVAL FACT

Dire wolves seemed to enjoy eating Ice Age horses.

Their remains have been found together at many fossil sites.

Xtreme Dire Wolf #2

A Sticky Situation California's La Brea Tar Pits trapped thousands of animals during the Ice Age. The animals died in the sticky liquid asphalt. About 90 percent of the remains found there belong to meat-eaters. Large plant-eaters got stuck in the asphalt. Meat-eaters entered the sticky lakes to grab them. Then they became stuck, too! Remains from more than 4,000 dire wolves have been found in the tar pits.

Dire wolves were mammals. Mammals have a backbone and fur and feed their babies milk.

Dire wolves lived from about 500,000 to 10,000 years ago.

Some researchers believe alpha males mated with all the females in the pack.

The largest dire wolves lived in the eastern United States. Most of them were found in Florida.

Like other canids, dire wolves had sharp teeth and strong jaws. They used them to slice through flesh and gnaw on bones.

Gray wolves and dire wolves existed in the same areas for about 400,000 years.

The dire wolf lived throughout North and South America.

One idea suggests that dire wolves' teeth were injured by hunting and fighting.

Dire wolves already existed in the Americas before gray wolves arrived.

Professor Joseph Leidy studied the first dire wolf fossil. He came up with the name *Canis dirus* in 1858.

Gray wolves came to North America from Asia. Land once connected the two continents.

Male and female dire wolves were about the same size. They were fully grown after one year.

Dire wolf packs included more than a dozen members. That is more than gray wolf packs.

Dire wolves had big heads, but they did not have